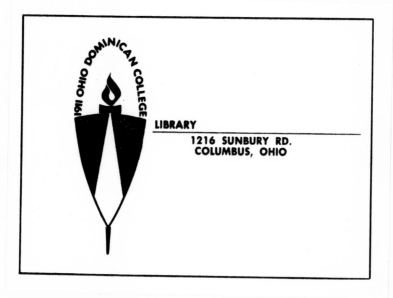

THANK YOU, FOG

THANK YOU, FOG
FOG
Last Poems by
W. H. AUDEN

RANDOM HOUSE NEW YORK

Grateful acknowledgement is made to the following
for permission to reprint previously published
material:

"Lullaby," "Address to the Beasts," "A Curse," and
"Nocturne" originally appeared in *The New Yorker*.
"Thank You, Fog" originally appeared in *Vogue*.
"Aubade" was first published in *The Atlantic
Monthly*.
"Archaeology," "Ode to Diencephalon," "Posthumous
Letter to Gilbert White," "No, Plato, No," "A
Thanksgiving," and "The Entertainment of the
Senses" originally appeared in *The New York
Review of Books*.

Library of Congress Cataloging in Publication Data

Auden, Wystan Hugh, 1907-1973.
    Thank you, fog.

    I. Title.
PR6001.U4T5   1974   821'.9'12   74-9049
ISBN 0-394-49496-2

Manufactured in the United States of America
First Edition

For MICHAEL and MARNY YATES

*None of us are as young
as we were. So what?
Friendship never ages.*

NOTE

When W. H. Auden died, on September 29, 1973, he had already gathered the poems in this book, together with its title and dedication. Had he lived, he would presumably have added sufficient poems to bring the book to about twice its present length before publishing it. As it stands, the book contains the poems that Auden completed after leaving New York in the spring of 1972 to return to his native England.

Two of the poems, however, are earlier. The lyrics written for a musical comedy based on *Don Quixote* date from 1963–64. Late in 1963 Auden and Chester Kallman were commissioned to prepare the libretto for *Man of La Mancha*, although the text eventually produced was entirely the work of others. Auden preserved these two fragments which he had written before leaving the project, and planned to publish them in this book. Although the typescript of the first bears the note "(I,29)," it evidently derives from a speech in chapter 11 of Part I of *Don Quixote*. The second is from a dialogue among Folly, Sin and Death, who were to comment on the main action of the play.

To the poems that Auden collected, the present volume adds Auden's last work for the stage, *The Entertainment of the Senses*, an antimasque written in September 1973, in collaboration with Chester Kallman. The Redcliffe Concerts of British Music, with funds provided by the Arts Council of Great Britain, commissioned the work as an interpolation for James Shirley's masque *Cupid and Death* (1653), and it received its first performance in London, at the Queen Elizabeth Hall, on February 2, 1974, with music by John Gardner.

The last poem that Auden wrote did not appear in the typescript of this book. It reads:

He still loves life
but O O O O how he wishes
the good Lord would take him.

EDWARD MENDELSON

CONTENTS

ix

THANK YOU, FOG

Thank You, Fog

Grown used to New York weather,
all too familiar with Smog,
You, Her unsullied Sister,
I'd quite forgotten and what
You bring to British winters:
now native knowledge returns.

Sworn foe to festination,
daunter of drivers and planes,
volants, of course, will curse You,
but how delighted I am
that You've been lured to visit
Wiltshire's witching countryside
for a whole week at Christmas,
that no one can scurry where
my cosmos is contracted
to an ancient manor-house
and four Selves, joined in friendship,
Jimmy, Tania, Sonia, Me.

3

Outdoors a shapeless silence,
for even those birds whose blood
is brisk enough to bid them
abide here all the year round,
like the merle and the mavis,
at Your cajoling refrain
their jocund interjections,
no cock considers a scream,
vaguely visible, tree-tops
rustle not but stay there, so
efficiently condensing
Your damp to definite drops.

Indoors specific spaces,
cosy, accommodate to
reminiscence and reading,
crosswords, affinities, fun:
refected by a sapid
supper and regaled by wine,
we sit in a glad circle,
each unaware of our own
nose but alert to the others,
making the most of it, for
how soon we must re-enter,
when lenient days are done,
the world of work and money
and minding our p's and q's.

No summer sun will ever
dismantle the global gloom
cast by the Daily Papers,
vomiting in slip-shod prose
the facts of filth and violence
that we're too dumb to prevent:
our earth's a sorry spot, but
for this special interim,
so restful yet so festive,
Thank You, Thank You, Thank You, Fog.

Aubade

(In Memoriam Eugen Rosentock-Huessy)

Beckoned anew to a World
where wishes alter nothing,
expelled from the padded cell
of Sleep and re-admitted
to involved Humanity,
again, as wrote Augustine,
I know that I am and will,
I am willing and knowing,
I will to be and to know,
facing in four directions,
outwards and inwards in Space,
observing and reflecting,
backwards and forwards through Time,
recalling and forecasting.

Out there, to the Heart, there are
no dehumanised Objects,
each one has its Proper Name,
there is no Neuter Gender:
Flowers fame their splendid shades,
Trees are proud of their posture,
Stones are delighted to lie
just where they are. Few bodies
comprehend, though, an order,
few can obey or rebel,
so, when they must be managed,
Love is no help: We must opt
to eye them as mere Others,
must count, weigh, measure, compel.

Within a Place, not of Names
but of Personal Pronouns,
where I hold council with Me
and recognise as present
Thou and Thou comprising We,
unmindful of the meinie,
all those We think of as They.
No voice is raised in quarrel,
but quietly We converse,
by turns relate tall stories,
at times just sit in silence,
and on fit occasion I
sing verses *sotto-voce*,
made on behalf of Us all.

But Time, the domain of Deeds,
calls for a complex Grammar
with many Moods and Tenses,
and prime the Imperative.
We are free to choose our paths
but choose We must, no matter
where they lead, and the tales We
tell of the Past must be true.
Human Time is a City
where each inhabitant has
a political duty
nobody else can perform,
made cogent by Her Motto:
Listen, Mortals, Lest Ye Die.

Unpredictable But Providential

(for Loren Eiseley)

Spring with its thrusting leaves and jargling birds is here again
to remind me again of the first real Event, the first
genuine Accident, of that Once when, once a tiny
corner of the cosmos had turned indulgent enough
to give it a sporting chance, some Original Substance,
immortal and self-sufficient, knowing only the blind
collision experience, had the sheer audacity
to become irritable, a Self requiring a World,
a Not-Self outside Itself from which to renew Itself,
with a new freedom, to grow, a new necessity, death.
Henceforth, for the animate, to last was to mean to change,
existing both for one's own sake and that of all others,
forever in jeopardy.
                The ponderous ice-dragons
performed their slow-motion ballet: continents cracked in half
and wobbled drunkenly over the waters: Gondwana
smashed head on into the under-belly of Asia.
But catastrophes only encouraged experiment.
As a rule, it was the fittest who perished, the mis-fits,

forced by failure to emigrate to unsettled niches, who
altered their structure and prospered. (Our own shrew-ancestor
was a Nobody, but still could take himself for granted,
with a poise our grandees will never acquire.)
                                                    Genetics
may explain shape, size and posture, but not why one physique
should be gifted to cogitate about cogitation,
divorcing Form from Matter, and fated to co-habit
on uneasy terms with its Image, dreading a double death,
a wisher, a maker of asymmetrical objects,
a linguist who is never at home in Nature's grammar.

Science, like Art, is fun, a playing with truths, and no game
should ever pretend to slay the heavy-lidded riddle,
What is the Good Life?
                                Common Sense warns me of course to buy
neither but, when I compare their rival Myths of Being,
bewigged Descartes looks more *outré* than the painted wizard.

Address to the Beasts

For us who, from the moment
we first are worlded,
lapse into disarray,

who seldom know exactly
what we are up to,
and, as a rule, don't want to,

what a joy to know,
even when we can't see or hear you,
that you are around,

though very few of you
find us worth looking at,
unless we come too close.

To you all scents are sacred
except our smell and those
we manufacture.

How promptly and ably
you execute Nature's policies,
and are never

lured into misconduct
except by some unlucky
chance imprinting.

Endowed from birth with good manners,
you wag no snobbish elbows,
don't leer,

don't look down your nostrils,
nor poke them into another
creature's business.

Your own habitations
are cosy and private, not
pretentious temples.

Of course, you have to take lives
to keep your own, but never
kill for applause.

Compared with even your greediest,
how Non-U
our hunting gentry seem.

Exempt from taxation,
you have never felt the need
to become literate,

but your oral cultures
have inspired our poets to pen
dulcet verses,

and, though unconscious of God,
your Sung Eucharists are
more hallowed than ours.

Instinct is commonly said
to rule you: I would call it
Common Sense.

If you cannot engender
a genius like Mozart,
neither can you

plague the earth
with brilliant sillies like Hegel
or clever nasties like Hobbes.

Shall we ever become adulted,
as you all soon do?
It seems unlikely.

Indeed, one balmy day,
we might well become,
not fossils, but vapour.

Distinct now,
in the end we shall join you
(how soon all corpses look alike),

but you exhibit no signs
of knowing that you are sentenced.
Now, could that be why

we upstarts are often
jealous of your innocence,
but never envious?

Archaeology

The archaeologist's spade
delves into dwellings
vacancied long ago,

unearthing evidence
of life-ways no one
would dream of leading now,

concerning which he has not much
to say that he can prove:
the lucky man!

Knowledge may have its purposes,
but guessing is always
more fun than knowing.

We do know that Man,
from fear or affection,
has always graved His dead.

What disastered a city,
volcanic effusion,
fluvial outrage,

or a human horde,
agog for slaves and glory,
is visually patent,

and we're pretty sure that,
as soon as palaces were built,
their rulers,

though gluttoned on sex
and blanded by flattery,
must often have yawned.

But do grain-pits signify
a year of famine?
Where a coin-series

peters out, should we infer
some major catastrophe?
Maybe. Maybe.

From murals and statues
we get a glimpse of what
the Old Ones bowed down to,

but cannot conceit
in what situations they blushed
or shrugged their shoulders.

Poets have learned us their myths,
but just how did They take them?
That's a stumper.

When Norsemen heard thunder,
did they seriously believe
Thor was hammering?

No, I'd say: I'd swear
that men have always lounged in myths
as Tall Stories,

that their real earnest
has been to grant excuses
for ritual actions.

Only in rites
can we renounce our oddities
and be truly entired.

Not that all rites
should be equally fonded:
some are abominable.

There's nothing the Crucified
would like less
than butchery to appease Him.

CODA

From Archaeology
one moral, at least, may be drawn,
to wit, that all

16

our school text-books lie.
What they call History
is nothing to vaunt of,

being made, as it is,
by the criminal in us:
goodness is timeless.

Progress?

Sessile, unseeing,
the Plant is wholly content
    with the Adjacent.

Mobilised, sighted,
the Beast can tell Here from There
    and Now from Not-Yet.

Talkative, anxious,
Man can picture the Absent
    and Non-Existent.

A Curse

Dark was that day when Diesel
conceived his grim engine that
begot you, vile invention,
more vicious, more criminal
than the camera even,
metallic monstrosity,
bale and bane of our Culture,
chief woe of our Commonweal.

How dare the Law prohibit
hashish and heroin yet
licence your use, who inflate
all weak inferior egos?
Their addicts only do harm
to their own lives: you poison
the lungs of the innocent,
your din dithers the peaceful,
and on choked roads hundreds must
daily die by chance-medley.

Nimble technicians, surely
you should hang your heads in shame.
Your wit works mighty wonders,
has landed men on the Moon,
replaced brains by computers,
and can smithy a "smart" bomb.
It is a crying scandal
that you cannot take the time
or be bothered to build us,
what sanity knows we need,
an odorless and noiseless
staid little electric brougham.

Ode to the Diencephalon

(after A. T. W. Simeons)

How *can* you be quite so uncouth? After sharing
the same skull for all these millennia, surely
you should have discovered the cortical *I* is
    a compulsive liar.

He has never learned you, it seems, about fig-leaves
or fire or ploughshares or vines or policemen,
that bolting or cringing can seldom earth a
    citizen's problems.

We are dared every day by guilty phobias,
nightmares of missing the bus or being laughed at,
but goose-flesh, the palpitations, the squitters
    won't flabbergast them.

When you could really help us, you don't. If only,
whenever the trumpet cries men to battle,
you would flash to their muscles the urgent order
    ACUTE LUMBAGO!

Shorts

Pascal should have been soothed, not scared by his infinite
     spaces:
God made the All so immense, stellar collisions are rare.

*   *   *

Earth's mishaps are not fatal,
Fire is not quenched by the dark,
no one can bottle a *Breeze*,
no friction wear out *Water*.

*   *   *

The conversations of birds
say very little,
but mean a great deal.

*   *   *

Butterflies, alas,
ignore us, but midges don't,
unfortunately.

*   *   *

When did the bed-bug
first discover
that we were tastier than bats?

*   *   *

Some beasts are dumb,
some voluble, but only
one species can stammer.

*   *   *

Among the mammals
only Man has ears
that can display no emotion.

*   *   *

Many creatures make nice noises,
but none, it seems,
are moved by music.

*   *   *

Beasts, Birds, Fish, Flowers do what
the Season insists They must,
but Man schedules the Days on
which He may do what He should.

*   *   *

Bound to ourselves for life,
we must learn how to
put up with each other.

*   *   *

Consciousness should be a parlour
where words are well-groomed
and reticent.

* * *

Man must either fall in love
with Someone or Something,
or else fall ill.

* * *

Nothing can be loved too much,
but all things can be loved
in the wrong way.

* * *

When truly brothers,
men don't sing in unison
but in harmony.

* * *

Whatever their personal faith,
all poets, as such,
are polytheists.

* * *

Envy we must those bards who compose in Italian or German:
    apposite Feminine Rhymes give them no bother at all.
We, though, thanks to a Tongue deprived of so many inflexions,
    can very easily turn Nouns, if we wish, into Verbs.

* * *

Met individually, most men appear friendly and gentle,
    but, collectively, Man commonly acts like a cad.

* * *

Policy ought to conform to Liberty, Law and Compassion,
but, as a rule, It obeys Selfishness, Vanity, Funk.

* * *

Where are brigands
most commonly to be found?
where boundaries converge.

* * *

Wherever there is gross
inequality, the Poor
corrupt the Rich.

Economics

In the Hungry Thirties
boys used to sell their bodies
for a square meal.

In the Affluent Sixties
they still did:
to meet Hire-Purchase Payments.

Posthumous Letter to Gilbert White

It's rather sad we can only meet people
whose dates overlap with ours, a real shame that
you and Thoreau (we know that he read you)
never shook hands. He was, we hear, a rabid

Anti-Clerical and quick-tempered, you the
quietest of curates, yet I think he might well have
found in you the Ideal Friend he wrote of
with such gusto, but never ran into.

Stationaries, both of you, but keen walkers,
chaste by nature and, it would seem, immune to
the beck of worldly power, kin spirits,
who found all creatures amusive, even

the tortoise in spite of its joyless stupors,
aspected the vagrant moods of the Weather,
from the modest conduct of fogs to
the coarse belch of thunder or the rainbow's

federal arch, what fun you'd have had surveying
two rival landscapes and their migrants, noting
the pitches owls hoot on, comparing
the echo-response of dactyls and spondees.

Selfishly, I, too, would have plumbed to know you:
I could have learned so much. I'm apt to fancy
myself as a lover of Nature,
but have no right to, really. How many

birds and plants can I spot? At most two dozen.
You might, though, have found such an ignoramus
a pesky bore. Time spared you that: I
have, though, thank God, the right to re-read you.

A Contrast

How broad-minded were Nature and My Parents
in appointing to My Personal City
exactly the sort of *Censor* I would have
    Myself elected,

Who bans from recall any painful image:
foul behaviour, whether by Myself or Others,
days of dejection, breakages, poor cooking,
    are suppressed promptly.

I do wish, though, They had assigned Me a less hostile
Public Prosecutor, Who in the early morning
cross-questions Me with unrelenting venom
    about My Future—

"How will You ever pay Your taxes?" "Where will You
find a cab?" "Won't Your Speech be a flop?"—and greets My
answers with sarcastic silence. Well, well, I
    must grin and bear it.

The Question

All of us believe
we were born of a virgin
(for who can imagine

his parents copulating?),
and cases are known
of pregnant Virgins.

But the Question remains:
from where did Christ get
that extra chromosome?

No, Plato, No

I can't imagine anything
   that I would less like to be
than a disincarnate Spirit,
   unable to chew or sip
or make contact with surfaces
   or breathe the scents of summer
or comprehend speech and music
   or gaze at what lies beyond.
No, God has placed me exactly
   where I'd have chosen to be:
the sub-lunar world is such fun,
   where Man is male or female
and gives Proper Names to all things.

   I can, however, conceive
that the organs Nature gave Me,
   my ductless glands, for instance,
slaving twenty-four hours a day
   with no show of resentment

to gratify Me, their Master,
    and keep Me in decent shape,
(not that I give them their orders,
    I wouldn't know what to yell),
dream of another existence
    than that they have known so far:
yes, it well could be that my Flesh
    is praying for "Him" to die,
so setting Her free to become
    irresponsible Matter.

Nocturne

(for E. R. Dodds)

Do squamous and squiggling fish,
down in their fireless houses,
notice nightfall? Perhaps not.
But any grounded goer,
and all to whom feathers grant
the sky's unbounded freedom,
alter their doings at dusk,
each obsequious to its
curiosity of kind.
The commons mild their movements
and mew all their senses, but
there are odd balls: for instance,
the owl and the pussy-cat,
as soon as day has thestered,
increase their thinking and jaunt
to kill or to engender.

No couple of our kindred
obey the same body-clock:
for most the law is to shut
their minds up before midnight,
but someone in the small hours,
for the money or love, is
always awake and at work.
Here young radicals plotting
to blow up a building, there
a frowning poet rifling
his memory's printer's-pie
to form some placent sentence,
and overhead wanderers
whirling hither and thither
in bellies of overbig
mosquitoes made of metal.

Over oceans, land-masses
and tree-tops the Moon now takes
her dander through the darkness,
to lenses a ruined world
lying in its own rubbish,
but still to the naked eye
the Icon of all mothers,
for never shall second thoughts
succumb our first-hand feelings,
our only redeeming charm,
our childish drive to wonder:
spaced about the firmament,
planets and constellations
still officiously declare
the glory of God, though known
to be uninfluential.

Out there still the Innocence
that we somehow freaked out of
where *can* and *ought* are the same:
so comely to our conscience,
where nothing may happen twice,
its timely repetitions,
so variant from our ways,
immodest scandal-mongers,
the way its fauna respect
the privacy of others.
How else shall mannerless minds
in ignorance imagine
the Mansion of Gentle Joy
it is our lot to look for,
where else weak wills find comfort
to dare the Dangerous Quest?

A Thanksgiving

When pre-pubescent I felt
that moorlands and woodlands were sacred:
people seemed rather profane.

Thus, when I started to verse,
I presently sat at the feet of
Hardy and *Thomas* and *Frost*.

Falling in love altered that,
now Someone, at least, was important:
Yeats was a help, so was *Graves*.

Then, without warning, the whole
Economy suddenly crumbled:
there, to instruct me, was *Brecht*.

Finally, hair-raising things
that Hitler and Stalin were doing
forced me to think about God.

Why was I sure they were wrong?
Wild *Kierkegaard*, *Williams* and *Lewis*
    guided me back to belief.

Now, as I mellow in years
and home in a bountiful landscape,
    Nature allures me again.

Who are the tutors I need?
Well, *Horace*, adroitest of makers,
    beeking in Tivoli, and

Goethe, devoted to stones,
who guessed that—he never could prove it—
    Newton led Science astray.

Fondly I ponder You all:
without You I couldn't have managed
    even my weakest of lines.

Lullaby

The din of work is subdued,
another day has westered
and mantling darkness arrived.
Peace! Peace! Devoid your portrait
of its vexations and rest.
Your daily round is done with,
you've gotten the garbage out,
answered some tiresome letters
and paid a bill by return,
all *frettolosamente*.
Now you have licence to lie,
naked, curled like a shrimplet,
jacent in bed, and enjoy
its cosy micro-climate:
Sing, Big Baby, sing lullay.

The old Greeks got it all wrong:
Narcissus is an oldie,
tamed by time, released at last
from lust for other bodies,
rational and reconciled.
For many years you envied
the hirsute, the he-man type.
No longer: now you fondle
your almost feminine flesh
with mettled satisfaction,
imagining that you are
sinless and all-sufficient,
snug in the den of yourself,
Madonna and *Bambino*:
Sing, Big Baby, sing lullay.

Let your last thinks all be thanks:
praise your parents who gave you
a Super-Ego of strength
that saves you so much bother,
digit friends and dear them all,
then pay fair attribution
to your age, to having been
born when you were. In boyhood
you were permitted to meet
beautiful old contraptions,
soon to be banished from earth,
saddle-tank loks, beam-engines
and over-shot waterwheels.
Yes, love, you have been lucky:
Sing, Big Baby, sing lullay.

Now for oblivion: let
the belly-mind take over
down below the diaphragm,
the domain of the Mothers,
They who guard the Sacred Gates,
without whose wordless warnings
soon the verbalising I
becomes a vicious despot,
lewd, incapable of love,
disdainful, status-hungry.
Should dreams haunt you, heed them not,
for all, both sweet and horrid,
are jokes in dubious taste,
too jejune to have truck with.
Sleep, Big Baby, sleep your fill.

TWO
DON QUIXOTE
LYRICS

The Golden Age

The poets tell us of an age of unalloyed felicity,
The Age of Gold, an age of love, of plenty and simplicity,
When summer lasted all the year and a perpetual greenery
Of lawns and woods and orchards made an eye-delighting
    scenery.

There was no pain or sickness then, no famine or calamity,
And men and beasts were not afraid but lived in perfect amity,
And every evening when the rooks were cawing from their
    rookery,
From every chimney rose the smell of some delicious cookery.

Then flowers bloomed and fruits grew ripe with effortless
    fertility,
And nymphs and shepherds danced all day in circles with
    agility;
Then every shepherd to his dear was ever true and amorous,
And nymphs of seventy and more were lovely still and
    glamorous.

O but alas!
Then it came to pass
The Enchanters came
Cold and old,
Making day gray
And the age of gold
Passed away,
For men fell
Under their spell,
Were doomed to gloom.
Joy fled,
There came instead
Grief, unbelief,
Lies, sighs,
Lust, mistrust,
Guile, bile,
Hearts grew unkind,
Minds blind,
Glum and numb,
Without hope or scope.
There was hate between states,
A life of strife,
Jails and wails,
Donts, wonts,
Cants, shants,
No face with grace,
None glad, all sad.

It shall not be! Enchanters, flee! I challenge you to battle me!
Your powers I with scorn defy, your spells shall never rattle me.
Don Quixote de la Mancha is coming to attend to you,
To smash you into smithereens and put a final end to you.

Recitative By Death

Ladies and gentlemen, you have made most remarkable
    Progress, and progress, I agree, is a boon;
You have built more automobiles than are parkable,
    Crashed the sound-barrier, and may very soon
    Be setting up juke-boxes on the Moon:
But I beg to remind you that, despite all that,
I, Death, still am and will always be Cosmocrat.

Still I sport with the young and daring; at my whim,
    The climber steps upon the rotten boulder,
The undertow catches boys as they swim,
    The speeder steers onto the slippery shoulder:
    With others I wait until they are older
Before assigning, according to my humor,
To one a coronary, to one a tumor.

Liberal my views upon religion and race;
　　Tax-posture, credit-rating, social ambition
Cut no ice with me. We shall meet face to face,
　　Despite the drugs and lies of your physician,
　　The costly euphemisms of the mortician:
Westchester matron and Bowery bum,
Both shall dance with me when I rattle my drum.

THE ENTERTAINMENT
OF THE SENSES

(by W. H. Auden and Chester Kallman)

The Entertainment of the Senses

CHAMBERLAIN

Ladies and gents,
Our troupe now presents:
THE ENTERTAINMENT OF THE SENSES.

FIRST APE

I'm Touch.
Touch me, touch me
If you'd smoothly learn much
How I've gone roughly free.

First of all, don't be touchy and take my advice:
Be intimate but not too nice.
Fidelity and all that
Has become old hat;
Today it's not done
To sleep with only one
And chastity's non-U.

49

Merely grab what is your due
And stroke it enough
With no prattle of love;
For Cupid, as Eros, you surely must know
If you're not old and silly,
Now presides over the Touch-and-Go
Of busy Piccadilly.
When you see a fair form, chase it
And if possible embrace it,
Be it a girl or a boy.
Don't be bashful: be brash, be fresh.
Life is short, so enjoy
Whatever contact your flesh
May at the moment crave:
There's no sex-life in the grave.

But when your hands make their sex tours
They may run into peculiar textures
Nature never quite thought of,
Wrought of
Coal-tar and spit
By brilliant hags
For keeping one fit
Without bumps, concavities, bulges or sags,
Much plastic, elastic and chilly
What-nots about willy-nilly;
And reaching for loot with a thief's
Dactyl dexterity you may steal upon briefs
Of genuine simulated seal-skin
And be flummuxed when chancing on real skin.
But if you're not sure
If they're meant to allure
Or only divert and protect,

For heaven's sake, do not object,
Since the Mode may be such,
And you mustn't lose touch:
No one cares what you think, but how you behave:
Lack of feeling is nothing, lack of touch very grave.

And there are many more new
Tactile sensations
Available to you
In developed nations,
And unknown to the peasant,
Not all of them pleasant:
If you handle a faulty switch
Your fingers may violently twitch
At the unexpected shock;
But we can't put back the clock.
On the whole we should clap
At the way things are going:
For comfort there's no competing
With Central Heating
And the joy of knowing
There's always hot water on tap.
Then on warm days now
You can cool your brow
With the breeze from an
Electric fan.
On Cupid's face there's a sensual grin
Because foam-baths have come in;
No cake of soap
Can ever hope
To provide so soft a lave:
It's a shame there'll be none in the grave.

Mild und leise
You'd be wiser
Not to be defenceless:
Nor walls nor fences
Can guard your senses—
Why not just be senseless?

SECOND APE

I'm Taste.
Taste me, taste me
In nutritional haste
For my new A.B.C.

Realize, since there is no disputing with Taste
That though oft violated, I always am chaste.
Nowadays you may carp that I'm not what I should be:
I am what I am when I am what I would be:
e.g. If I were a herb I'd be evenly branched,
Born crispy and gold, I'd be powdered and blanched,
As a wine I'd be water and wolf's blood, and if
I were tropical fish I'd arrive frozen stiff,
If I were a chick I'd be battery-fed,
And if I were a sponge I'd be sliced up as bread.
If I were a meal that was meant to seduce
A male into marriage, I'd moan "What's the use?"
Feed the Beast, I have heard, but what slips to his belly
Doesn't matter too much when he's glued to the Telly;
And if I had intentions more directly erotic,
I'd remember that Cupid's gone macrobiotic;
Though his too-divine packaging rouse appetite,
It won't show that his palate has gone with his sight.

But were I just myself, I'd meet woe in this Hall,
For how could I sing being nothing at all?
So I'll be a burnt roast, and if my guests are meanies
Who dote on their food, they'll get *six* Dry Martinis;
And I'll don heavy clogs and dance several jigs on
Dear Elizabeth David and darling Jane Grigson:
Oh they're wonderful ladies, but will make a fuss
About opening tins, not at all, girls, like us.
The poor cranks may complain I'm a nerveless dull bitch—
They're just jealous because I'm so vitamin-rich:
And if *you* think me insipid, unnatural and coy,
You can dowse me in ketchup or souse me with soy.
As for *her*, hungry Nature, that well-seasoned tart
Who arrives uninvited and consumes A-La-Carte,
Let her bring her own Glutamate with if she's smart:
After all she's just there to corrupt and deprave
When she dines upon gamey old you in the grave.

ALL FIVE

Mild und leise, etc.

THIRD APE

I'm Smell.
Smell me, smell me
To be sure you can tell
What a chic smell should be.

Let's say you're a woman, going out for the best:
First of all, I suggest
That Pro-Lib or Anti, you should and you can
Start with your arm-pits and shave like a man.

53

Then douche, dab and diddle because, dear, you know
That *Bachelor's-Offer* isn't short for B.O.
And the gent who awaits you, never mind what it costs,
Will have taken precaution against fumes and exhausts;
Though he forgets the aroma of wine would
Be drowned by his smokes, that is not your affair:
He will reek like an acre of pine-wood
To show you and Cupid how much he could care.
Well,
Swell—
But what now of you, and how should you smell?
There's fragrance of course in the blooms of the wood,
But for Nature to give you the aroma she should
For you to get on and get off in,
You'll need more bouquets than they put on a coffin:
So be well-advised
Now you're de-odorised
And reach for a scent that you chose
Because, though worn out by assault, your own nose
Twitched at it because it was well-synthesised.
And with the vernal voice of the turtle *I* sing
When I pray
You—now spray
Yourself as though you were fertilising
The passive eggs of a fish;
And the creature you hatch
Can now swish
To make a fine catch
Safely downstream,
The exotic,
Narcotic
Whiff of a dream,
A for-the-few, not-the-many thing,

54

A pound, not a penny thing,
Oh!
So
If you want power, affection and pelf,
Sweet, smell like anything
Except yourself.
But if you're mad to be natural and personal, save
Your money and be Mother Nature's unspoilable slave:
She'll see that you stink like us all in the grave.

ALL FIVE

Mild und leise, etc.

FOURTH APE

I'm hearing.
Hear me, hear me
Prove you pure noise endearing
As it now is to me.

When Life seems dreary, Oh
Switch on your Stereo
And turn the volume to high:
Soft music makes us cry.
The songs of birds may be seraphic
But, however sweet, they can't compete
With the roar of city traffic
Or the stentorian sound
Of a Jet-plane leaving the ground.
So when you motor-bike
Down the M.1. or its like,
Imagine you're late—

Accelerate, accelerate,
Show your decibel power
At a hundred an hour.
It's no longer a sin
To make a din
Since that, until lately
Unknown, unstately
God, Cacophony
Made his Theophany;
And Cupid, bored by peace and quiet,
Only aims to cause a riot.
So, lovers, fill your lungs
And let go with your tongues
To talk, talk, talk, talk
With your Transistors on as you walk.
For the prissy minority
Who prefer a low sonority
There's only one thing to be done:
Become a Trappist or a Nun.
Let them. Come, girls and boys,
More noise, more noise!
Yell while you can and save
Your silence for the grave.

ALL FIVE

Mild und leise, etc.

FIFTH APE

I'm Sight.
See me, see me
Make the scene a delight
In life optically.

A mountain, we must confess, is
No longer a surprise;
What really impresses
Contemporary eyes
Are the vertical escarpments
Of High-rise Apartments:
Each rectangular block
Makes Gothic or Baroque
Look over-complicated,
Their cathedrals out-dated.
Then already the printed word
Is beginning to seem absurd;
It's so easy to misconstrue,
And far too many do.
Now only a snob
Would take on the job
Of scanning a book
When he could look
At life up close and so real on
Telly from San Francisco to Ceylon.
But, if his fancy leans
To Fiction, Movies tell
The tallest stories well,
And there are Fashion Ads
In glossy magazines—
Long-haired lassies and lads
All shot in shocking color—
Black and white was so much duller.
It's a new world, so make sure
Should you go on tour
To Greece or New York or the Fens,
To be in the swing:
Never look at a thing

Except through a camera lens.
Yes, we're lucky: whereas
As soon as the sun withdrew
Our forebears had to make do
With candles or with gas,
We have the felicity
To possess electricity,
Can lighten our rooms
And dispel the Glooms
With lots and lots
Of bulbs of at least a hundred watts.
And Cupid, called blind,
You will find
Is only short-sighted
And likes life well-lighted,
Preferring to know
At just whom he is aiming his bow:
Candles that splutter
And very soon gutter
Remind him of Plato's cave
And the blindness of the grave.

ALL FIVE (Stretto)

Though our views be reprehensible
To you and indefensible,
Please admit they're comprehensible
And, naturally, sensible.
        Good-bye!
When you get a little older
You'll discover like Isolde:
"We must love one another *and* die!"

(Enter *Death* from behind, unseen by the others.
He folds his arms and looks on.)

CHAMBERLAIN

Dear listeners, you have heard tonight
What my five apes have had to say
About our senses five,
Through which we know we are alive:
Touch and Taste and Smell
As well as Hearing and Sight,
And the different roles they play
Now as compared with yesterday.
Cupid, the god, would certainly nod,
And you'll all agree, I'm sure, with me
That they are perfectly right.
The moral is, as they have said:
Be with-it, with-it, with-it till you're dead.

ABOUT THE AUTHOR

WYSTAN HUGH AUDEN was born in York, England, in 1907. He came to the United States in 1939, and became an American citizen in 1946. Educated at Gresham's School, Holt, and at Christ Church, Oxford, he was associated with a small group of young writers in London—among them Stephen Spender and Christopher Isherwood—who became recognized as the most promising of the new generation in English letters. He collaborated with Isherwood on the plays *The Dog Beneath the Skin, The Ascent of F6,* and *On the Frontier,* as well as on *Journey to a War,* a prose record of experiences in China. He edited many anthologies, including *The Oxford Book of Light Verse* and, with Norman Holmes Pearson, *Poets of the English Language.* In collaboration with Chester Kallman, he also wrote the libretti for Igor Stravinsky's opera *The Rake's Progress,* and for Hans Henze's opera *Elegy for Young Lovers.* His selected essays, *The Dyer's Hand,* appeared in 1962. *Academic Graffiti,* with illustrations by Filippo Sanjust, appeared in 1972.

W. H. Auden is the author of several volumes of poetry, including *The Double Man, For the Time Being, The Age of Anxiety, Nones,* and *The Shield of Achilles,* which received the National Book Award in 1956. His most recent collections of poetry are *City Without Walls* (1969) and *Epistle to a Godson* (1972).

In 1972 Mr. Auden returned to Oxford, where he resided at Christ Church as an honorary student. He died in 1973.